Old BARNARD CASTLE

by
Charles Lilley B.Sc., C.Eng., M.I.Gas E.

Bede Terrace South was an insular group of residential properties, the first of three rows of housing that were later renamed collectively as Bede Road. Here two main roads, the Stockton to Barnard Castle turnpike from the east, and the Sunderland Bridge to Bowes Turnpike from the north, merged. Many of the premises boarded summer visitors. Today the area in the foreground is covered in housing, but apart from the maturing of the trees and removal of the iron railings, the terrace has changed little in 100 years.

© Charles Lilley 2000
First published in the United Kingdom, 2000,
by Stenlake Publishing, Ochiltree Sawmill, The Lade,
Ochiltree, Ayrshire, KA18 2NX
Telephone / Fax: 01290 423114

ISBN 1 84033 105 4

THE PUBLISHERS REGRET THAT THEY CANNOT SUPPLY
COPIES OF ANY PICTURES FEATURED IN THIS BOOK.

FURTHER READING

The books listed below were used by the author during his research. None of them are available from Stenlake Publishing. Those interested in finding out more are advised to contact their local bookshop or reference library.

R. P. Wright, *Archaeologia Aeliana*, XIV, 1937.
R. W. Atkinson, *Barnard Castle & its Neighbourhood*.
Denis Coggins, *Teesdale in Old Photographs*, 1989.
Parkin Raine, *Teesdale in Old Photographs, Second Selection*, 1994.
Douglas M. Ramsden, *Teesdale*, 1947.
C. P. Nicholson, *Teesdale Handy Guide – series 5*, 1921.
C. Lilley, *Parish Church of St Mary, Barnard Castle*, 1999.
The *Teesdale Mercury*.
Teesdale Record Society transactions, 1934-1946.

ACKNOWLEDGEMENTS

Particularly to Mrs L. Eden (p 26); L. Nelson (pp 4, 22, 46); Newsquest (N.E.) Ltd. (p 12); Mrs F. Parker (pp 27 & 45); P. Raine (pp 40 & 42); Mrs M. Wallis (p 10) for the supply of pictures, and the other local people who have donated copies or original postcards.

Now No. 1 Cambridge Terrace, this late Victorian property was the home of Mr M. Murray, the local 'Man from the Pru', when this picture showing him, his wife and two daughters was taken in 1909. Constructed from local stone, the building is typical of the residential properties that were built in the upper part of the town. So, too, are the garden walls and iron railings, although the latter were removed during World War II for scrap metal. A major change in building materials is evident in the use of imported blue slate for roofing in place of the more expensive local sandstone slabs that would have been used previously.

INTRODUCTION

Barnard Castle, 'Barney' to its residents, is a market town on the north bank of the River Tees in south-west Durham. There is no evidence of permanent settlement in the area until the twelfth century, although the occasional find of stone tools and weapons indicates the presence of man some 3,000 years ago or more. By AD 79 the Roman army had advanced into the north of England, later establishing their presence with forts four miles south at Lavatrae, the modern-day village of Bowes, and four miles south-east, at Greta Bridge. It was from the former camp that a Roman road led north-east, crossing the Tees by ford to join Dere Street near Bishop Auckland.

Prior to the Norman Conquest, the upper half of Teesdale was already combined into an Anglo-Norse estate centred upon the ancient village of Gainford, mortgaged to the Earls of Northumberland by Aldhun, the Bishop of Durham. In 1080, following the killing of Walcher, the first Norman Bishop of Durham, the countryside was laid to waste by the Normans. A further rebellion in 1095 by Robert Mowbray, the Norman Earl of Northumbria, induced William II to break the earldom up into smaller baronies. Of these, he gave the lordship of Gainford to Guy de Baliol. Defensive needs required the removal of the lord's residence from Gainford, eight miles west, to a high rocky scar overlooking the Tees, adjacent to the river crossing of the old Roman road from Bowes. Guy de Baliol's small earthwork castle was rebuilt in stone by his successor Bernard Baliol I. In time a small gathering of dwellings was built around the castle, the residents being only too glad of the protection it provided against the onslaught of Scottish marauders. These Norman burgesses' plots formed the basis of the main streets of Barnard Castle still evident today.

By the thirteenth century, the number of inhabitants attracted to the new administrative centre of Teesdale were such that Barnard Castle's population outstripped its parochial parent village of Gainford. Charters had been given to the town by the early Baliols, first around 1160 and again by 1250. The endowment of St John's Hospital had been founded by John Baliol, ancestor to a later John, King of Scotland. Religious needs were met by enlargement to the chapelry, additions of chantries to both the town and castle chapels, and, by 1381, by the grant for the foundation of an Augustinian friary by Thomas Beauchamp, Earl of Warwick. Agriculture, together with the woollen and leather industries, thrived.

In 1569 the Rising of the North saw the siege of the castle, with Sir George Bowes holding possession of the fortifications for eleven days, delaying the insurgents until the advance of the Earls of Warwick and Surrey contributed to the speedy suppression of the rebellion. The castle had by this time passed its peak and the fortifications began a rapid decay. By 1630 the building had been stripped of its roofing, lead, and timbers. Encroachment of housing had begun adjacent to the castle moat, and this became a common sewer.

The eighteenth and nineteenth centuries saw the introduction of the manufacture of flax products such as thread, shoelaces and rope, and the woollen industry provided the basis for a growing carpet industry. The Tees supplied both the working power and the necessary medium for the dyes. The area between the western walls of the castle and the river became the industrial centre of the town, with the majority of the workers drawn from Bridgegate and Thorngate and their complex of yards. This workforce subsisted in conditions which led in 1849 to the outbreak of Asiatic cholera.

Despite the appalling living conditions in the lower parts of the town, the surrounding countryside had sufficient appeal to attract early visitors, amongst them Charles Dickens, Sir Walter Scott, and the artists Turner and Glover. Introduction of the railways in 1856 opened the area to a wider group of holidaymakers, as Teesdale became within a day's reach of any part of the country. To accommodate the visitors the town expanded to the north and east, with the provision of fine stone-built houses and shops along Galgate (the route of the old Roman Road) and Newgate. It was in the latter street that the town's 'Jewel in the crown', The Bowes Museum, was built, although its opening in 1892 came long after the deaths of the founders. In 1885 a group of cyclists from Tyneside chose the town as the centre for its annual Meets each Whitsuntide, and although the cyclists' association with the Meet ceased between the wars, the event, despite having encountered many difficulties, still survives in revised form each Spring Bank Holiday weekend.

Barnard Castle continued its military associations after the demise of the castle. The Durham Militia was founded in the town in 1759, and it later became the headquarters of the 3rd Battalion of the Durham Light Infantry. During World War I, the 17th Battalion DLI was a training and recruiting source for dispersal of personnel to sister battalions. Annual camps had long been held across the river on Deerbolt Park, later to become a permanent camp during World War II, together with other camps to the north of the town.

Throughout its history, Barnard Castle's main role was – and still is – as a market town for the surrounding agricultural area of Teesdale. Each aspect of this had its own specific area, with livestock towards Galgate, and the mixed market within Market Place overspilling to the upper part of The Bank. In 1747, Thomas Breaks provided the Market Cross to provide protection for farmers' wives selling dairy produce and poultry. Today, the military connections have gone, and the woollen and leather trades have vanished, along with the majority of their associated buildings. The main commercial areas now have modern shopfronts, although close examination of the upper stories reveals little change to the fine Georgian and Victorian buildings over the past 100 years.

As early as 1833 representations had been made by the residents of the town to the Stockton & Darlington Railway for a branch line to Barnard Castle and Teesdale. An Act of Parliament of 1845, permitting extension of the railway from Bishop Auckland, was never enacted due to financial difficulties and private dissension. A further Act, introduced in 1853, was rejected by Parliament, mainly because of the objections of major landowners and the turnpike trustees. By 1854 approval had been obtained, and the Darlington to Barnard Castle line opened in 1856, terminating immediately behind upper Galgate. The continuation of the line in 1861 across Stainmore to Tebay required the resiting of the passenger station half a mile to the north. Further extensions, with lines to Bishop Auckland in 1863, and Middleton-in-Teesdale in 1868, required the addition of two bay platforms at each end of the station. Here, a train awaits departure in the west bay.

Following resiting of the passenger station, the original building was relegated to use as the goods station, and the fine frontal portico was removed to Saltburn as a memorial to the Prince Consort, where it remains. The four-gabled frontage of the 'new' station is illustrated here. With six passenger trains each day over Stainmore Summit to and from Darlington, services to Bishop Auckland (some of which continued to Middleton), and extensive mineral traffic, the station became very lively. Local hotels provided transport to their individual hostelries for visitors, and the vehicle in the picture is Smith's omnibus of the King's Head Hotel, photographed c.1900.

This photograph of the north-west side of Galgate was taken shortly after the building of the Holy Trinity Methodist Church in 1894 (its spire is visible in the distance on the left). Galgate is the northern approach to the town, and was built on the line of the Roman road from Bowes to Binchester. As Barnard Castle's population grew in the late nineteenth century, the more genteel members of society moved northwards from the lower parts of the town to new dwellings along Galgate and the streets bordering it. Commercial enterprises soon followed, with the conversion of the ground floors of some of these properties. The postman is standing outside premises that are undergoing conversion, and which were subsequently used by E. A. Metcalfe, a photographer. The property beyond with three bay windows was converted to shop frontage soon after this picture was taken.

This view shows further incursion of retail properties into the former domestic architecture of Galgate. Mr Metcalfe the photographer has been and gone, his former premises occupied in 1925 by Dalston Cycles. Three shopfronts fill the place of the bay windows, while the railed enclosure contains the Boer War Memorial. The main road is to the left of the photograph. Being the principal approach to the town from the north for visitors arriving by both road and rail, this was improved in the 1880s by the planting of trees and addition of flower beds with ornamental railings.

There is no postmark on this card to provide a date, but the shadows would indicate a summer mid-morning, and the occasion is likely to have been the procession that followed the church service on 19 July 1919 to commemorate the end of World War I. The cortege includes members of the fire brigade, district councils and various adult and youth groups.

Soldiers of the 3rd Battalion DLI in dress uniform, with mounted officer behind, leave the wider section of Galgate. Are they the rearguard of the previous procession? Predominantly youths, the cadre contains a few mature faces, probably those of experienced combatants in the previous hostilities. Close inspection of the background reveals a number of motor cars, which were beginning to challenge horse transport by this time.

For many years the wider section of lower Galgate was the site of livestock markets, although these were eventually moved to the purpose-built mart in Vere Road. One survivor of the livestock trade in this location was the twice-yearly horse fair which continued into the 1940s. For some time the lower right room of the house to the left in this picture was used as the office of S. A. Tait, the gasworks manager. The placards on the wall were timetables for United Services buses.

The Durham Light Infantry, in dress uniform of red tunics with green facings, stand to attention at the Trooping of the Colours on the morning of 9 July 1914, prior to marching to St Mary's Parish Church for the laying-up of the old colours of the 4th Battalion. At the rear, standing on the tiered pavement, a large congregation has gathered to watch the occasion, as future crowds were to do at similar ceremonies until the late 1950s. The 'pant' or fountain, complete with ornamental gas lamp, was erected for Queen Victoria's Jubilee in 1874.

With five or more regiments garrisoned around the town, Galgate remained a popular venue for army parades into the late 1950s, the wide carriageway and service roads providing excellent facilities for the functions. In 1954, one such regiment was Beating the Retreat, again watched by a large crowd. Amongst the spectators, many of whom are still resident in the town, one young lady carries her sister on her back. Her personal burden became, some ten years later, the author!

5720, HORSE MARKET. BARNARD CASTLE.

Looking back from Horse Market towards Galgate. The three-storey house in the distance on the right (now the post office), was at one time the home of a Durham Militia surgeon called Munroe. The only vehicle in this 1920s picture is a car parked outside Will Harris's poultry & fish shop. Mr T. Garbutt's drapery business, with ornate lamp, is in the second of three locations in the town (see page 22.) The former Star Hotel is now the site of a bakery.

Market Place, Barnard Castle.

The market in full swing, with carts parked up and horses stabled for the day. The premises on the left occupy the sites of the former burgesses' plots laid out in the twelfth century, the land behind reaching to the old Back Lane (now Queen Street). These long back yards, reached by individual passageways, soon had domestic premises and stabling built on them. The buildings on the right were seventeenth century additions, the area originally being open ground to the moat and castle walls.

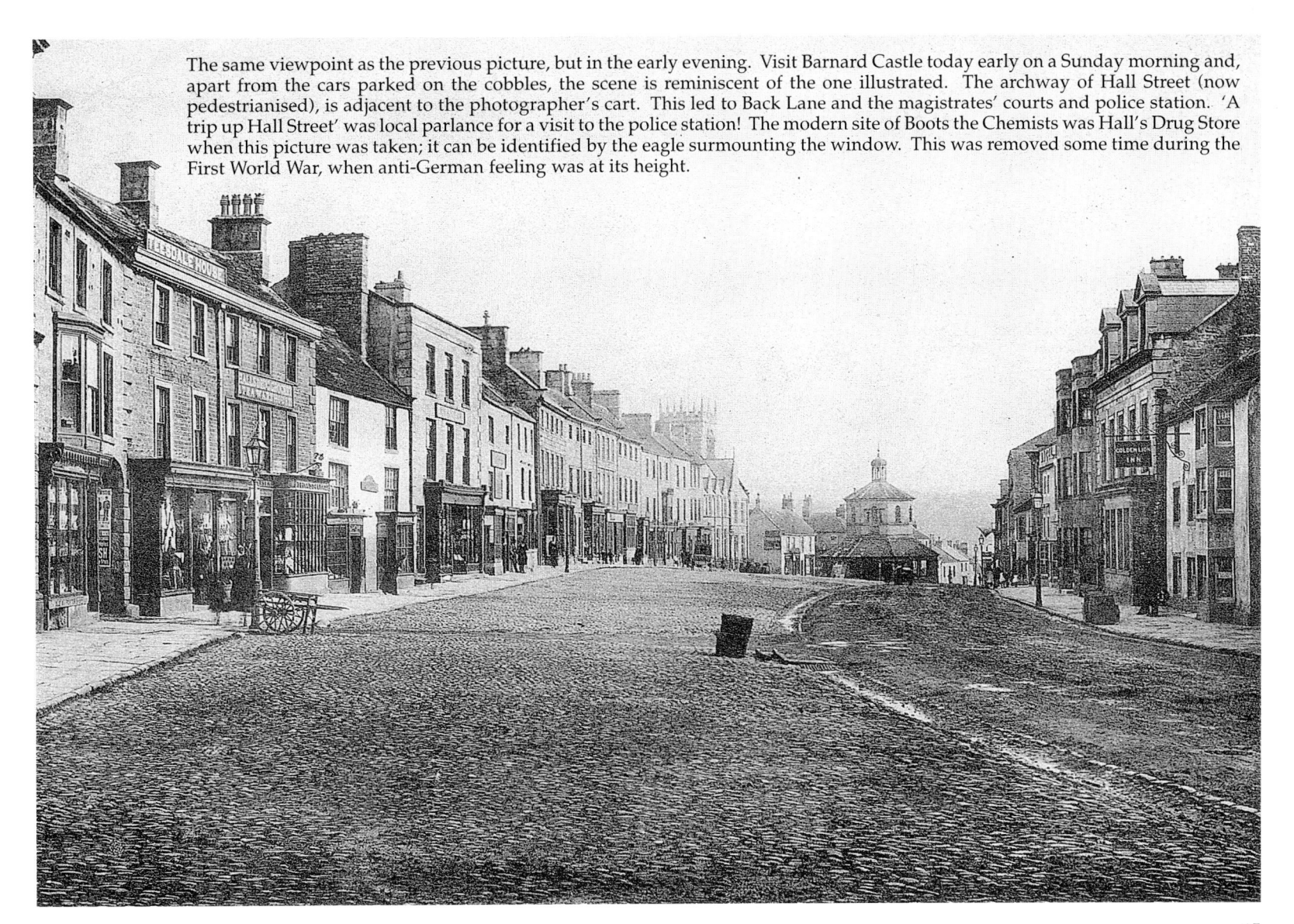

The same viewpoint as the previous picture, but in the early evening. Visit Barnard Castle today early on a Sunday morning and, apart from the cars parked on the cobbles, the scene is reminiscent of the one illustrated. The archway of Hall Street (now pedestrianised), is adjacent to the photographer's cart. This led to Back Lane and the magistrates' courts and police station. 'A trip up Hall Street' was local parlance for a visit to the police station! The modern site of Boots the Chemists was Hall's Drug Store when this picture was taken; it can be identified by the eagle surmounting the window. This was removed some time during the First World War, when anti-German feeling was at its height.

The young lady is standing outside the National Provincial Bank c.1900, which before being rebuilt as the bank was the home of the Hanby family. The shop window directly behind is surmounted by ornamental ironwork, which was once widespread throughout the town centre, but sadly has only been retained by one shop. In the left background a horse and cart stands near the shop of Thomas Humphrey, clock maker; the nearby Raby Hotel was formerly the town house of the Lords Barnard. The white building in the centre background is Amen Corner, in the far half of which Thomas Humphrey's shop was previously located. The window of the chemist's, above the handcart on the left, is surmounted by a bust. (The handcart stands outside Lloyd's Bank, which replaced the former Bluestone House, a Tudor-style building not unlike Blagraves.)

This picture of the Red Lion in Market Place appears to have been commissioned by a Mr Jackson, with six reproductions costing the princely sum of 7s 6d. The rendered stone building was roofed in local sandstone slabs, and the clothing of the two gents would suggest the picture was taken in the 1930s. By the early sixties the building had been demolished, and the site is now occupied by modern premises that are totally out of character with the remaining buildings. The passageway to the right gave access to one of the many yards that lay behind Market Place. The large arch on the left formed part of the extended King's Head, and gave access to the castle via the site of the long gone Town Gate.

Early morning and a party of young ladies departs for a local excursion, watched by a window cleaner perched on the bay window of the original section of the King's Head Hotel. Below him a lady passes with a bundle of laundry. The oval plaque on the wall to the right of the window cleaner bore the insignia of the North of England Cycling Club, while the plate high above him on the left was the building's fire insurance plaque. Charles Dickens stayed in the King's Head in 1838 while investigating Yorkshire schools in preparation for his novel *Nicholas Nickleby*.

The King's Head showing the imposing extension that was added in the late 1800s on the site of the former Queen's Head Hotel. The portion on the left is the original coaching inn, which formerly had four bay windows and a low arch. The old arch led into what was known as Castle Wynd, and was removed some time in the mid-nineteenth century, thereby improving access to the coachbuilders situated directly behind the hotel. Hannah Hall's grocery and flour shop is at the extreme right of the picture.

Two individuals, one of them leaning on a shooting stick, discuss the day's topics outside Finlay's shop at Amen Corner *c.*1918. The imposing building on the corner was Backhouse's Bank, built in 1877 in place of much older shops. The octagonal building is the Market Cross, wrongly called the Butter Market by outsiders and the misinformed. In fact the butter market was one event that took place within it, not the building itself. The central portion of the Market Cross, a donation of Thomas Breaks, was built in 1774 and is made up of a piazza enclosed with iron railings. This was later encased with timber and glazed panels. The Cross has served many purposes: as the venue for the sale of dairy produce, live poultry and rabbits; a court house with lockup below; the town hall (following demolition of the Shambles); a surveyors office; and the fire station. Surmounted with a cupola which was renovated in 1999, it is topped by a weather vane bearing two musket ball holes inflicted in 1804.

The Market Cross looking west from Newgate. The picture was obviously taken on a Wednesday – with the overspill from the market spreading to The Bank – and dates from c.1930. Market traders' baskets and crates lean against the screen partitions of the Cross. The gable end of Amen Corner provides a convenient location for advertisements for the Wycliffe Cinema, the 'House of Mystery' (Blagraves), and LNER local and regional timetables. With the advent of the motor vehicle and increased traffic, it became necessary to widen the junction, and Amen Corner was demolished.

1933, and Amen Corner is reduced to rubble. During demolition the interior plaster was found to contain stems of hemlock, which was used as both binding material and to prevent against vermin infestation! Commerce House, occupied by Thomas Garbutt, drapers, was demolished some fifty years later. The site stood vacant for a considerable period before a new housing development, in a style sympathetic with the surroundings, was built in its place. Changes in modes of transport are still taking place, with horse-power and motor car, both with accompanying trailers, visible in the picture.

The substantial church of St Mary's has had only eleven vicars in its 800 year history. This is because prior to 1866 it was a chapel within the parish of Gainford, served by a curate. This view of the church from the south-east *c.*1900 shows it much as it appears today, although the pinnacles on the chancel and nave have been removed, and the gravestones realigned. The building was restored in 1870 and the old tower replaced in 1873. In the right background is the spire of the Unitarian Church, later used by the Church of England as a church hall. It was demolished in 1957 and replaced by the existing church hall.

Amen Corner from The Bank. A mixed crowd watches a contingent of the DLI entering the cobbled approach to St Mary's Parish Church around the time of the First World War. Watson's had previously been the shop of Thomas Humphrey, remembered in *Master Humphrey's Clock*, written by Charles Dickens on his visit to the town 75 years earlier.

A challenge for the town's older residents – name those faces! This solemn group from the Church of England Boys School was photographed in 1921. William Banks, in his final year as headmaster at the time, appears to have been camera shy, along with the other teachers. Three of the pupils are wearing scout uniforms. Sited at the south-east corner of the churchyard, the school was rebuilt in 1892 and replaced the much earlier National School building. Following removal of the school to the northern end of the town, its buildings stood empty for some time prior to conversion into flats.

The single-storey building on the right is the thirteenth century St John's Hospital, founded in Newgate by John Baliol for the maintenance of thirteen poor women under the wardenship of a chantry priest. As an ecclesiastic foundation, and therefore of 'superstitious nature', it was subject to the Chantry Surveys of Henry VIII and Edward VI, but owing to its charitable nature was allowed to continue under the guardianship of an appointed master. Poor administration of its assets resulted in a serious loss of revenue, and by 1863 only one bedeswoman was resident. The building was demolished in 1965. The larger building to the left was used by the Congregational Church as a Sunday school.

During the nineteenth century several dissenting churches were established in the town. The Congregational Church began a Sunday school in Newgate in 1803, and following several moves eventually acquired a site in Back Lane at the junction of Hall Street large enough for the construction of the existing church, presbytery and a new school room (illustrated here).

Six months into the First World War and posters 'Call to the men of Teesdale' to enlist in the Volunteer Training Corps. These two volunteers, still in their teens, together with a passing youngster acting as temporary bell-ringer, pose outside the new Drill Hall in Birch Road. The hall, still in existence, was built within 200 yards of the barracks of the 4th Battalion DLI, and later became the depot of the local contingent of the 6th (Territorial) Battalion. It was subsequently used by the YMCA, and is currently home to Barnard Castle Rugby Club. Enlistment into the regular army would have been via the 17th Battalion DLI, formed in 1915 for initial training prior to transfer to one of the many fighting battalions overseas.

This imposing piece of Parisian-style architecture, transposed into the Teesdale landscape on the east of Barnard Castle, must come as something of a shock to the unsuspecting visitor. The Josephine & John Bowes Museum was begun in 1869 and was intended to serve both as one of their residences, and as the home for their large and varied collection of antiquities. Josephine, Countess Montalbo, died in 1874 and her husband in 1885. A legacy left by John Bowes enabled the museum and park to be opened to the public in 1892. As an added attraction, a bandstand of cast iron was formally opened in July 1912 by Lady Glamis. By the early 1950s, lack of use, and its interference in the site lines required for a performance of *Merry England*, required the bandstand's removal. The incomplete 'chapel in the park' is visible on the right, with the old Militia barracks to the left. The two fields immediately behind the museum were used as the site for much-needed council housing in 1936 and 1947.

In addition to the bandstand, other amenities within the Bowes Museum Park included the bowling green and tennis courts, provided in 1908 and separated by a common sports pavilion. The remains of the Roman Catholic chapel, which was commenced in 1875, are in the background. The building was never completed due to a lack of access to the church whilst the park was closed. Resiting it at the south-west corner of the park in 1926, where direct access could be obtained from the junction of Newgate and Birch Road, solved the access problem. Stone from the old building was recovered for construction of the new chapel, and was transported to the site by a small purpose-built tramway. The site of the old chapel was converted into a putting green, now long gone. At the far corner of the bowling green, locals may recall a tall cylindrical stone post box.

There is a series of at least four postcards relating to the landing of this RE8 biplane on the Upper Demesnes in 1917. After leaving Newcastle en route to Leeds on 30 March, the aircraft ran out of fuel over Barnard Castle. Official supervision of the plane was necessary while it was on the ground, particularly as it remained in this location overnight, and the Volunteer Training Corp provided the required security (not the dog, although he does look the more intimidating!). The following day a large crowd gathered to witness the plane taking off. A similar event took place in the early 1950s when a light aircraft landed at the same location, again attracting the attention of local school children.

This postcard was a chance find, hidden amongst those of Newcastle-upon-Tyne. Whilst the insignia of Tyne Cyclists Club was misleading for the postcard dealer, the lower shield consisting of cross, crescent and estoile is instantly recognisable to most Barney locals, and the picture is typical of the North Eastern Cyclists Meet. A note on the reverse of the card reads 'Whit 1913 – This is our working staff, taken on Whit Tuesday, before the decorations were taken down'. The heavy decoration has obliterated almost all architectural features of the building, but the alternating black and white quoin-stones are a feature of only one building in Barnard Castle. Behind the portrait of George V at first floor level on the right, the street sign for Market Place can be made out. The premises stand at No. 2, and are those of Morton's Restaurant, directly opposite the Market Cross. During the Meet each cycling club had its own HQ, and the challenge of putting up the best decorations was highly competitive. Whilst the cycling aspect diminished during and after the First World War, the Meet is still a popular annual attraction, with a fair, fancy dress parade and other more modern events.

Of the two local cycling clubs, the Teesdale Wanderers and the Barnard Castle Excelsior Cyclists Club, the latter chose the Burns Head Inn as its HQ. There are a series of photographs of the inn decorated for the Meets between the two World Wars, when among the hosts were Matthew Gash and Tom Merryweather. One of the Excelsior's captains, R. G. Jackson, the proprietor of a nearby cycle shop, became the first local man to hold the office of President of the Meet in 1934.

The staff of the post office at No. 11 The Bank, some time around 1916. The premises were formerly Ascough's, and are now Connelly's toy shop. Apart from a change in the glazing, the frontage of the property remains much the same today. Recruitment of soldiers was of paramount importance at the time, as illustrated by the enlistment posters showing various branches of the British Army. The post office has been situated in five or more different locations, and this is at least the third place it stood at. It had previously been sited in Bridgegate and Newgate, then moved from the above location to Horse Market, and finally to its present location in Galgate. Note the bands on the uniforms signifying degrees of seniority.

MARKET CROSS,
BARNARD CASTLE.

The continuation of Market Place, interrupted only by the presence of the Cross, is The Bank. Presenting little difficulty to modern traffic, the slope was such that a heavy cart drawn by a single horse needed to take a zigzag course while ascending the hill. On occasions the descent probably caused some consternation too. The old post office, shown in the previous photograph, is just out of view to the left.

Blagraves House, named after a former owner, is the oldest surviving domestic building in Barnard Castle, and tradition says that Oliver Cromwell was entertained here when he visited the town in October 1648. The building has served many purposes and borne many names. At one time it was the Boar's Head Inn; then a museum, 'The House of Mystery'; and later a cafe called the Cromwell Restaurant. Broadgates, one of the town's five gates, stands to the right of the building. The sign adjacent to the front door reads 'J. Kavanagh, (late Brass) – Rope Maker', indicating the building's use at the time. There are many illustrations of the interior, particularly when Blagraves was used as a museum. In this case the stone-vaulted cellar is labelled the 'torture chamber'.

This picture of The Bank from near the junction of Bridgegate and Thorngate shows the mix of domestic and commercial premises in this area. The stone-faced building on the right incorporating the archway was the Steward's or Manor House. The arch gave access into Wycliffe Yard, where in addition to domestic premises a fine Wesleyan chapel was sited. This was later converted into the Wycliffe Cinema, referred to on a sign in the picture on page 21. The single-storey building at the extreme left, previously roofed with 'black thack' (ling thatching), was demolished in 1901 to make way for the new Church Mission. Priory Yard was situated beyond the houses on the right. Its name derived from an Augustinian friary founded around 1200 ('priory' appears to be a corruption of 'friary'). The friary building was demolished long ago, but during reconstruction of various surrounding premises medieval timber-work was revealed.

A shopkeeper suns himself in a chair placed in the roadway near the junction of The Bank and Grey Lane, which provided access to the Lower Demesnes. Opposite is the narrow entrance to Bridgegate. The white building on the corner was demolished to permit easier access for increased motor traffic. Whilst outwardly they look like eighteenth century buildings, many of the neighbouring properties contain structural walls and timbering from much earlier periods.

Formerly fine residential dwellings, the majority of these buildings in Thorngate were converted into tenements, and in many the top floor windows were altered to provide increased light for weavers who worked from their homes. The three-storey mansion partly obscured by the bull-nosed Morris and sycamore was the former home of Judge Hullock, Baron of the Exchequer. His affluence would have contrasted sharply with life in the nearby poorhouse, which was situated to the rear of the houses on the extreme right and not, as quoted in a recent publication, forming part of St John's Hospital. During the late 1950s a large proportion of the old housing in the Bridgegate and Thorngate area was demolished to make way for new local authority housing. Fortunately, several properties were acquired by the Teesdale Buildings Preservation Trust and sympathetically restored.

Behind the frontages of Bridgegate, known locally as Briggate, were the many yards where the greater proportion of the town's population subsisted in conditions which led to the outbreak of Asiatic cholera in 1849. 369 residents in a population of 4,350 contracted the disease, of which 132 resided in the properties of Bridgegate and 154 within Thorngate. Whilst sanitation improved, conditions were such that during the early twentieth century the incidence of TB within the area was twice the national average. Clearance of the premises was undertaken and only two of the original buildings now remain.

This late nineteenth century view by Elijah Yeoman, taken from across the Tees in Startforth, shows the densely occupied area behind the buildings on the left of the previous photograph which was the centre of the majority of cases of cholera fifty years earlier. Several tall chimneys indicate the reason for the derelict state of the weir, steam power having arrived and superseded the use of water as a source of power. By this time, however, the carpet industry had already ceased, hence the reason that some properties are derelict and without roofs. Despite this, many of the houses were still occupied over fifty years later.

Like the railway, the gasworks came late to Barnard Castle, with Darlington, Richmond and Northallerton having had works for several years before they were established in the town in 1835. Raby Castle even boasted a gas-lit theatrical performance some 20 years earlier. The gasworks were built where an old beck approached the Tees within a deep gully to the north-west of the castle. During extensions in 1839 when a second gas holder was built, the Roman road from Bowes to Binchester was uncovered skirting the gully. Later extensions in 1885 for the provision of a third gas holder (nearest the camera in this picture) uncovered a further section of the limestone roadway. Mr Yeoman was very selective when taking this picture of the castle, in that a large holly tree was used to obscure the rather unaesthetic gasworks. This is particularly regrettable as there are virtually no pictures of the works. Their main gate is visible to the right of the bush with the gable end of the purifier house, which was subsequently extended. The second and third of the four gas holders (not gasometers) can be seen to the left of the tree, although there were only ever two on the site at any one time. The further-away of the two holders, demolished by the 1930s, was of cast iron construction and incorporated counterweights. The author's father, later the works' foreman, was employed here from 1933 until his retirement in 1977. His eldest son left school in 1947, aged 14, and at 10 o'clock that very night was stoking the retorts!

The heart of all gasworks was the retort house. Here, coal was heated in horizontal retorts of refractory material to around 1000° F, yielding the gaseous by-products and gas itself, which were delivered by vertical pipework to a pneumatic main running the full length of the retort benches. The picture shows a bench of two sets of six retorts being renovated with, to the right, an almost completed setting of six retorts, requiring only the replacement of the cast iron doors and ascension pipes. The setting to the left still requires the installation of the flues and retorts.

The 1891 original of this Yeoman gasworks photograph hung inside the governor-house building for about 70 years, disappearing some time around 1957! It was possibly discarded by the first non-engineering manager, but fortunately one copy survived for posterity. The new town governors, constructed by Brian Donkin of Chesterfield, have been installed and the enclosing governor-house building is shown under construction by local masons, one being a great-great uncle of the author. The retort house is to the rear beyond the main gate, with the stores and fitters building, originally the manager's house, behind. To the right is the gable end of the purifier shed. Today, the governors have gone, the gasworks too, and even the Donkin Company has closed. The governor-house is now the only structure remaining on the site.

Taken from the Water Bridge, this photograph shows the castle beyond the Warrens Dam, which provided the driving force for Ullathorne's Flax Mill. The dam appears to be under repair as a set of sheerlegs are visible to the left of the dam wall. Beyond these the gasworks can be seen hidden within the trees, with the boiler-house chimney protruding. The scar on the river bank was created by the tipping of the retort house ash at a time when the river was considered a suitable place for disposing of any sort of refuse.

From the dress of these young ladies, sitting at the northern side of Warrens Dam, the picture would appear to date from the 1920s. The Tees Valley and Cleveland Water Board aqueduct, known as the Water Bridge, is in the background. Built in 1893, the aqueduct conducted water from the reservoirs on the Rivers Lune and Balder to the large conurbations of Stockton and Middlesbrough. The water authority permitted use of the bridge for public access. After falling into disrepair the dam was removed and reconstructed.

Members of the DLI at an annual camp during World War I at Deerbolt Park on the Yorkshire side of the river, seated for a group photograph which includes two members of the local Barker family. With children and a number of civilians present, attention seems to be drawn to the group's right, where other troops are apparently parading. The recruitment demands of the war required the formation of training battalions including the 17th DLI, which was formed in 1915 and billeted under canvas on the camp field. During World War II the site was used for the construction of one of several permanent army camps, and is currently the site of a young offenders institution.

This large industrial complex on the south bank of the Tees opposite Barney was known as Bridge End Mills, and was part of the international company of Ullathorne & Langstaff. Originally it was powered by a water mill driven by the outfall from Warren Dam. Commenced in 1760, the undertaking eventually became the town's largest employer, with over 400 workers. Later converting to steam power, the factory supplied shoe thread, ropes and twine. By the early twentieth century, foreign competition had reduced the workforce to 100 employees, and the mill closed in 1931. Demolished in 1976, the site was cleared with only the base of the chimney and remnants of the sluice-gate gearing remaining.

The Tees takes a sharp turn to the east as it passes Thorngate Mill. The Thorngate Dam can be seen crossing the river diagonally towards the mill race, and immediately to the left of the mill, adjacent to the river bank, the white plumes of the race overspill are visible. The main feed water emerged just to the left of the chimney. The smaller building to the right of the footbridge was always powered by steam, hence the presence of the chimney. Surplus steam was piped across the bridge approach (the support girders are just visible between the buildings) for use in the other part of the mill. The stack of Ullathorne's Mill in the far distance and the other buildings of the riverside complex chart the demise of water power. Within a few years of the closing of the mill, the dam had fallen into disrepair, frequent flooding having removed all but a small section of masonry which remains hidden in the shrubbery on the Durham bank.

There are photographic records of very few of the many yards which existed throughout the town, and certainly none taken by professional photographers, since the yards were hardly photogenic and pictures of them had no commercial value. It was left to residents using a prized Box Brownie to record family occasions, and hopefully the background too. I am only aware of two other photographs of yards that have been published apart from this one, which was taken from the family album and shows a yard off Market Place. The year is 1944 and the location Linton's Yard. The names of these yards changed frequently, along with the owner or occupant of the premises adjacent to the entrance passageway. Previously the same yard was recorded as Putnam's. I knew it as Eastwood's Yard, but locals may remember it more recently as Waistell's, and now Boots. In the picture the author's mother takes time off from housework and part-time employment, whilst 'yours truly' considers another foraging trip through the door to his right – into the greengrocers warehouse – for a further supply of fresh green peas! Living in this location gave one a special advantage, when, months later, bananas became available. The rear building with built-up arch was previously Cross House, the former home of William Smith the foundry owner, and later became part of the now demolished Low Mill.